LET'S DRAW ANIMALS

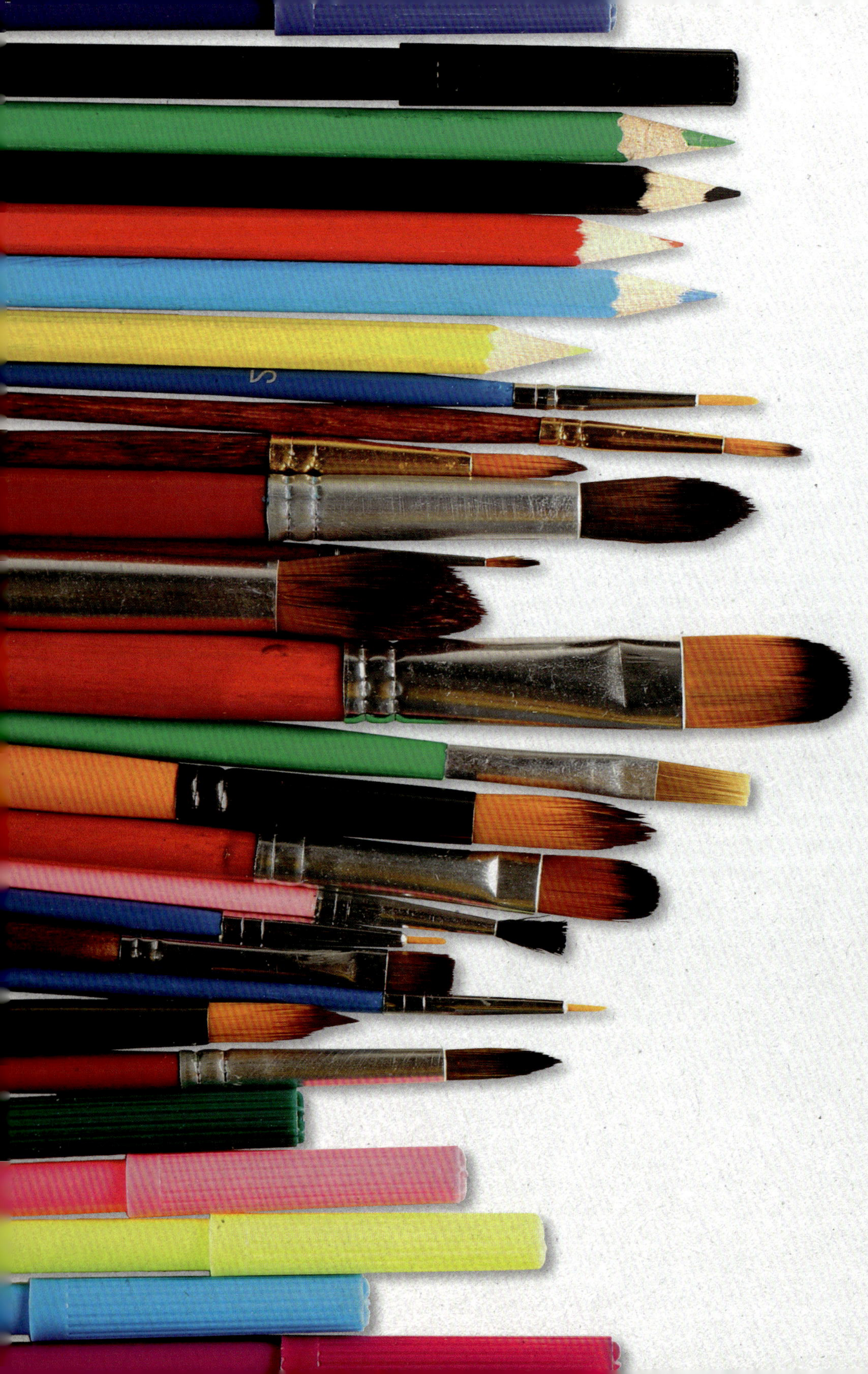

Reycraft Books
145 Huguenot Street
New Rochelle, NY 10801

reycraftbooks.com

Reycraft Books is a trade imprint and trademark of Newmark Learning, LLC.

Library of Congress Control Number: 2022914967

Hardcover ISBN: 978-1-4788-8185-8
Paperback ISBN: 978-1-4788-7044-9

Photo Credits: Inside Back Jacket B, Page 3A: subjug/Getty Images; Book Spine, Jacket Spine: pixhook/ Getty Images; Page ii, iii, iv: ArtSvetlana/Shutterstock; Page 2: xpixel/Shutterstock; Page 3B: studiovin/ Shutterstock; Page 5: ; Page 7: ; Page 9: Courtesy of Carole Pope; Page 11: ; Page 13: Courtesy of Wook Jin Jung; Page 15: ; Page 17: ; Page 19: Courtesy of. Huan-Hong Wu; Page 21: Photograph by Stephen Kennedy; Page 23: Courtesy of Ken Ko; Page 25: Courtesy of Javier RamÃrez; Page 27: Courtesy of Kyle Beckett; Page 29: Courtesy of Wu, I-Chien; Page 31: ;All other images from Shutterstock

Printed in Dongguan, China. 949559/0525/22906

10 9 8 7 6 5 4 3 2

First Edition published by Reycraft Books 2023.

Reycraft Books and Newmark Learning, LLC support diversity and the First Amendment, and celebrate the right to read.

LET'S DRAW ANIMALS!

Fifteen of your favorite illustrators have come together to help make drawing animals a little easier. Drawing should be fun! Everyone has their own style, so don't forget—there's no need to be perfect! So if you make a mistake, don't worry. Erase or start fresh on a new piece of paper. It takes a lot of practice to become an artist, so keep at it and eventually you'll draw just the way you want!

Every artist has their own special way of working. Some start with a pencil sketch on paper and color it with paint or markers. Others use a computer or tablet with a stylus to make their drawings. Some use both. Use what you have and what feels right. The options are endless! Combining different methods and materials can often produce beautiful and unexpected results. There are no rules when being creative. Give in to your imagination. Study the artists' step-by-step directions, try their helpful tips, and get started. Are you ready? Let's draw animals!

LET'S DRAW AN ELEPHANT . . .

1.

2.

3.

4.

5.

RAQUEL BONITA

TIPS AND TRICKS...

✔ If you split any figure into simple geometric shapes, you can draw anything.

✔ You can try different types of eyes to give your characters unique and funny expressions.

LET'S DRAW A HIPPO . . .

1.

2.

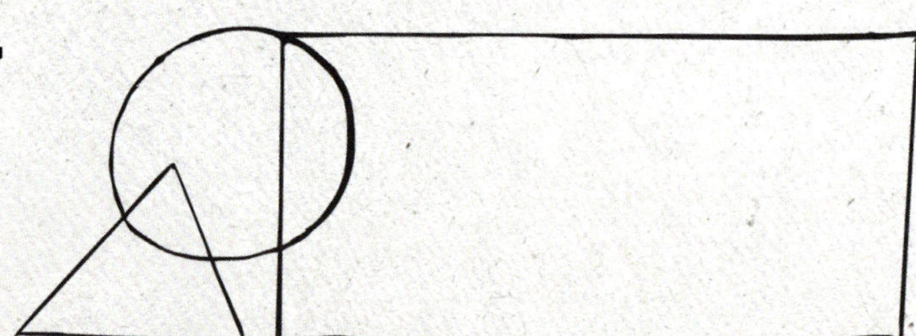

3.

4.

5.

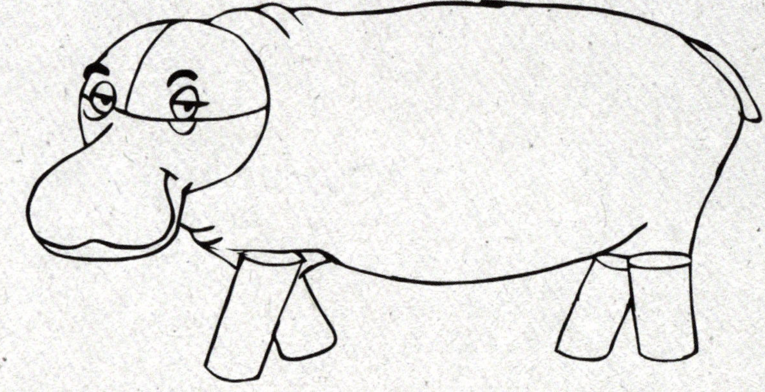

6.

7.

8.

HENRY EZEOKEKE

TIPS AND TRICKS...

- ✔ Start with simple shapes like a circle, rectangle, triangle, or cylinder.
- ✔ Create an eye line and center line in the middle of the circle and triangle.
- ✔ Soften the hard edges of the rectangle and triangle into curves to create the hippo's body.

LET'S DRAW A GIRAFFE . . .

1.

2.

3.

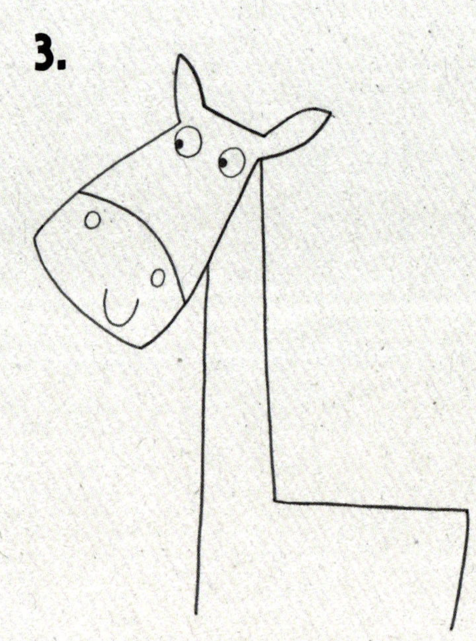

4.

5.

6.

TIPS AND TRICKS...

- ✔ Giraffes each have their own unique spot pattern. Squeeze in more if you like! Make some big and some small.
- ✔ Giraffes are the tallest mammals in the world. You can always make the neck even longer!

LET'S DRAW A GORILLA . . .

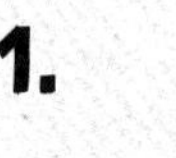

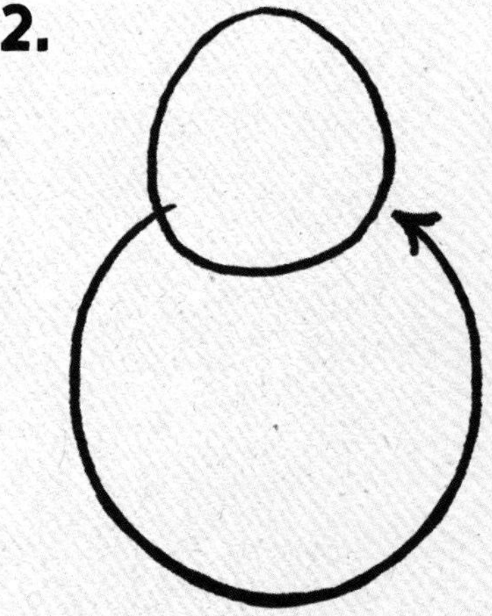

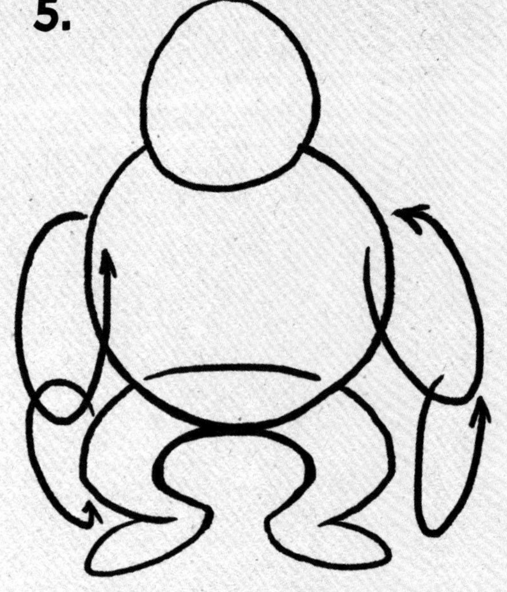

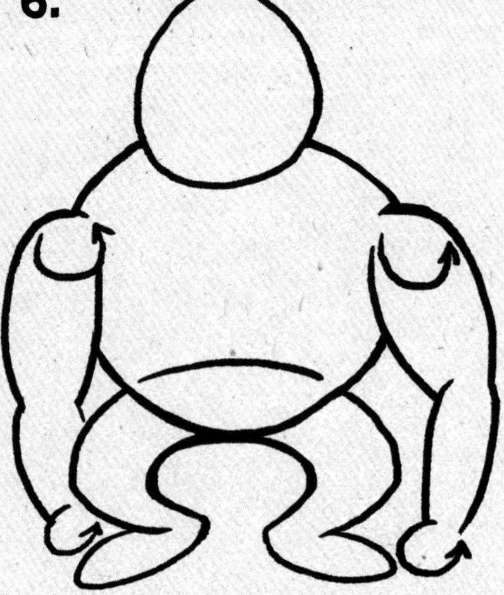

7.

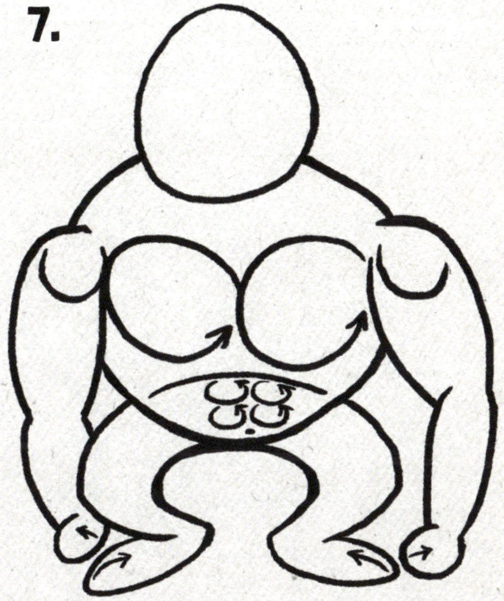

8.

9.

CHUCK GONZALES

TIPS AND TRICKS...

- ✔ Always start with a light sketch so you can figure out the basic shapes of the figure before making darker lines.
- ✔ Highlights can make drawings and paintings pop. Put highlights at the highest point of an object where the light would hit it.

LET'S DRAW A CAT . . .

1.

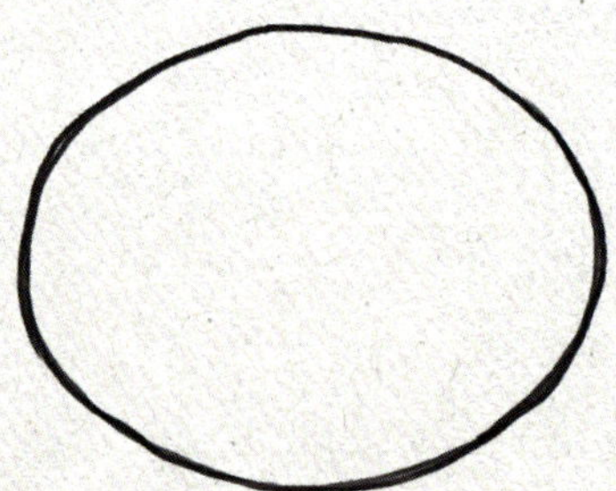

2.

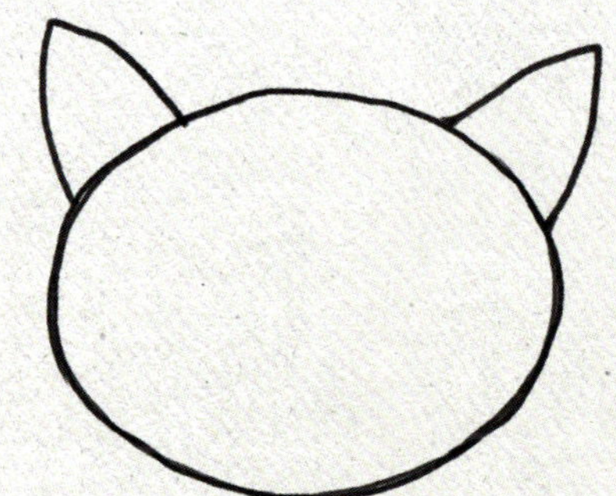

3.

4.

5.

6.

7.

8.

WOOK JIN JUNG

TIPS AND TRICKS...

- ✔ When you draw a cat's eyes, remember that a cat's pupils are vertical (tall and narrow) and shaped like a grain of rice, unlike people.
- ✔ Don't forget to add whiskers and patterns on the cat's body and face. Also, make sure that the ears are pointy!

LET'S DRAW A BEAR . . .

1.

2.

3.

4.

5.

6.

TIPS AND TRICKS...

- ✔ The littlest bit of shading can give your art so much dimension. Sometimes less is so much more!
- ✔ See that plate of fish? Swap it out for a basketball or a birthday cake. Bam! You've got a whole new story.

LET'S DRAW A JAGUAR . . .

1.

2.

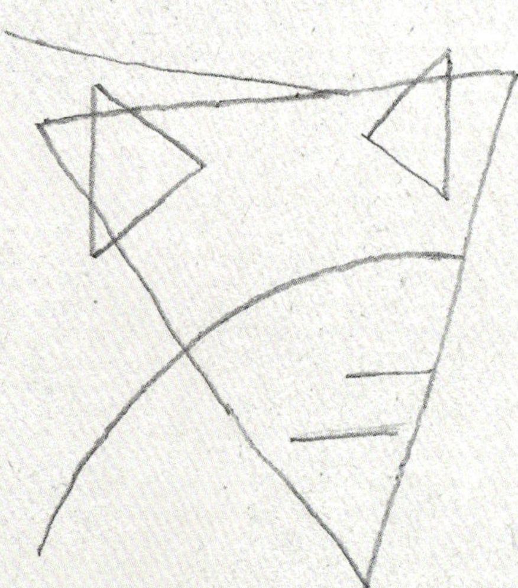

3.

4.

5.

6.

COLIN BOOTMAN

TIPS AND TRICKS...

- ✔ At the beginning of each drawing, make sure your pencil strokes are light. A light drawing allows you to easily correct mistakes over time.
- ✔ Start your drawing by using shapes that you are already familiar with. Common shapes are circles, triangles, rectangles, straight lines, curved lines, and angled lines.

LET'S DRAW A DUCK . . .

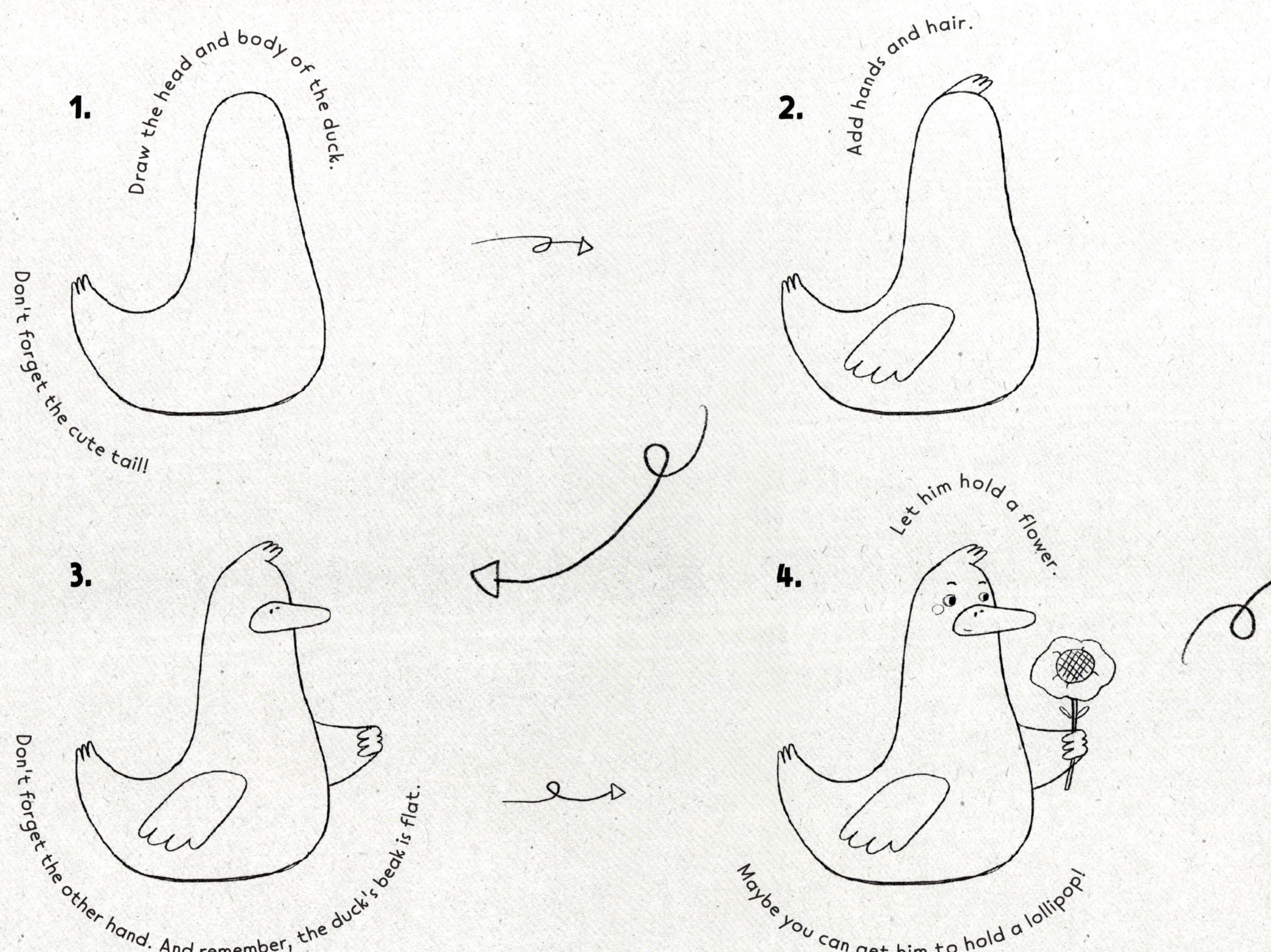

LIAN AN-LIN
6.
Ducks can swim in the water and walk on the road!
5.
Give him a warm scarf.
It's almost done! You can add feet so he can walk on the ground!

LET'S DRAW A BIRD . . .

1.

2.

3.

4.

5.

6.

7.

CBABI BAYOC

TIPS AND TRICKS...

✔ Don't get so hung up on the proportions. Variation is a great way to add uniqueness.

✔ A consistent light source helps give the character more dimension and life.

LET'S DRAW A RABBIT . . .

1.

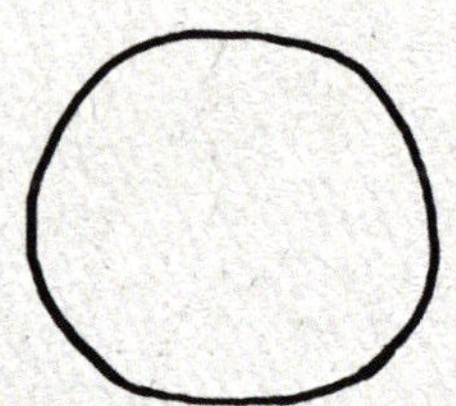

3.

4.

MORI

TIPS AND TRICKS...

✔ The ears of the rabbit can be as dramatic as you want! Keep this in mind, and let your imagination guide you.

✔ Don't forget to decorate your rabbit. Holding a carrot? Tying a bow? This can make your rabbit come alive.

LET'S DRAW A MONSTER . . .

1.

2.

3.

4.

5.

6.

SR. RENY

TIPS AND TRICKS...

- ✔ Add lots of eyes and spots. It will make the monster weirder and scarier.
- ✔ Be creative and use your favorite color combination. That will help you create a one-of-a-kind monster.

LET'S DRAW A DOG . . .

1.

2.

3.

4.

5.

6.

KYLE BECKETT

TIPS AND TRICKS...

- ✔ A dog's snout can be as long or short as you'd like it to be.
- ✔ You can always change the ears of a dog. They can be short and pointy, or long and floppy.
- ✔ Try drawing two or three dogs with different patterns, snouts, and ears.

LET'S DRAW A CROCODILE . . .

1.

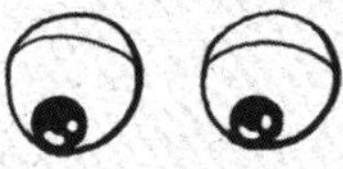

2.

3.

4.

5.

6.

JOYCE SUN

TIPS AND TRICKS...

- ✔ The long jaw is the main feature of the crocodile. You may choose to keep it open or closed. An open jaw will look fierce!
- ✔ Change the alligator's shape or angle and get a totally different look and feel. Try it and you'll see.

LET'S DRAW A DRAGON . . .

1.

2.

3.

4.

5.

6.

7.

HECTOR BORLASCA

TIPS AND TRICKS...

- ✔ You can change the dragon's color. Green can be perfect, too!
- ✔ Try to add a flare near the dragon's mouth and you can make a fire dragon!

Be sure to check out all these other titles from Reycraft Books, illustrated by the artists from *Let's Draw Animals!*

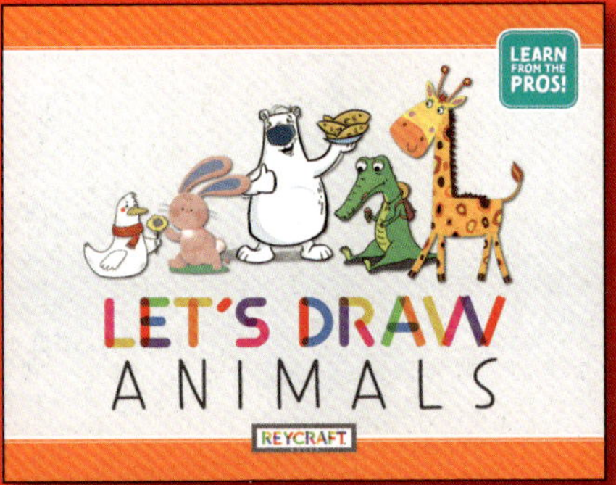

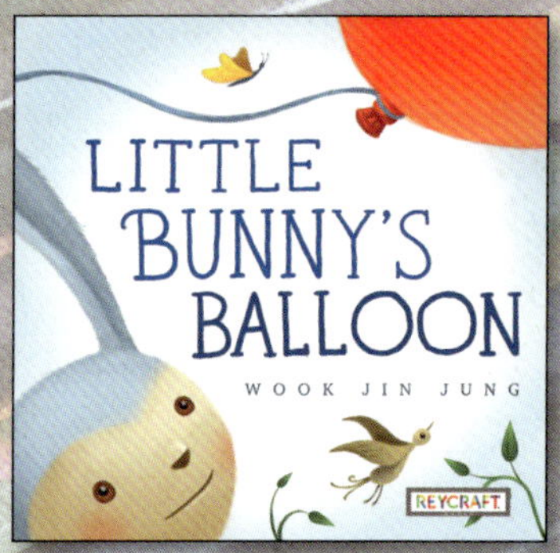

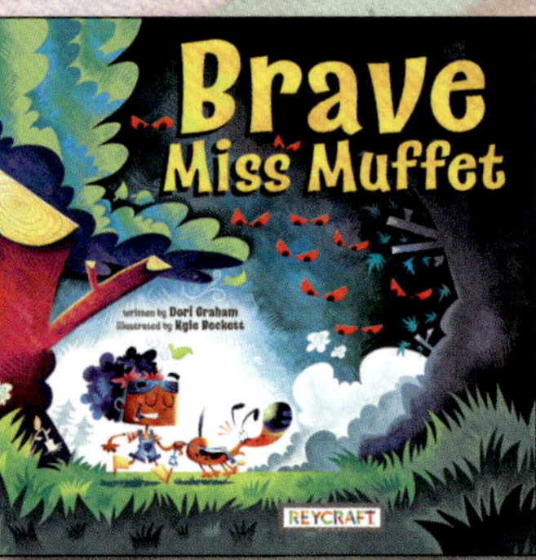

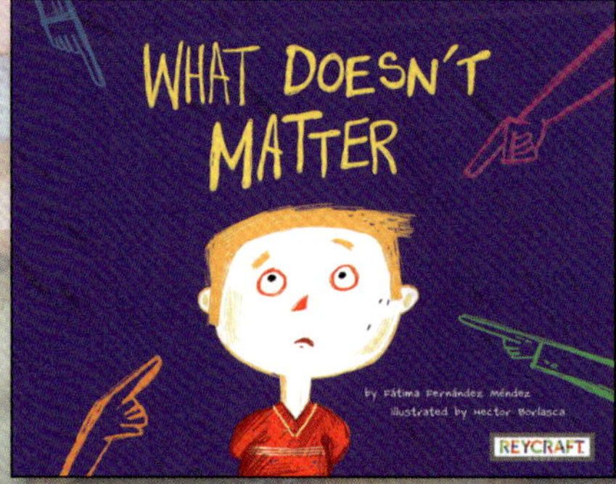

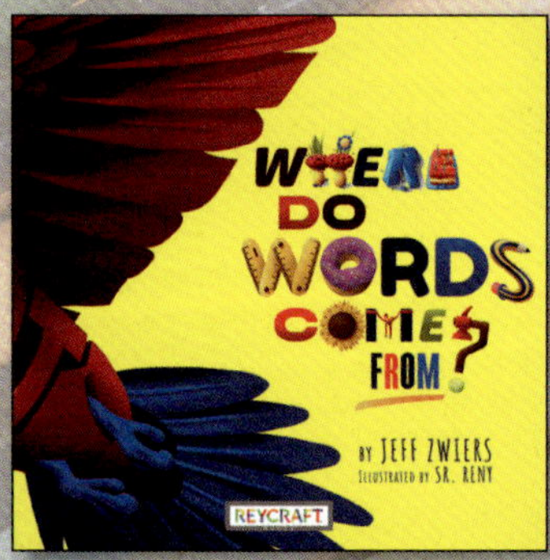

REYCRAFT
BOOKS
reycraftbooks.com